Alexander Graham Bell

A. Roy Petrie

Fitzhenry & Whiteside Limited

Contents

Chapter		Page
1	Death Strikes	3
2	Family Tree	7
3	Wonders of Speech	10
4	A New Home	15
5	Experiments in Sound	19
6	First Phones	27
7	Phones Go Far	32
8	Other Phones	39
9	Sallies into Medicine	43
10	Into the Air	47
11	Onto the Water	58
12	Citizen of the World	62
	Reference, Credits, Index	64

THE CANADIANS
A Continuing Series

Alexander Graham Bell

Author: A. Roy Petrie
Design: Kerry Designs
Cover Illustration: John Mardon

Canadian Cataloguing in Publication Data
Petrie, A. Roy (Auldham Roy), 1921-1979.
Alexander Graham Bell
(The Canadians)
Bibliography: P. 64
ISBN 1-55041-463-1
1. Bell, Alexander Graham, 1847-1922. 2. Inventors - Canada - Biography.
3. Inventors - United States - Biography. I. Title. II. Series
TK6143.B4P47 1992   621.385'092   C92-095039-6

Revised Edition
Printed and bound in Canada.
ISBN 1-55041-463-1

© 1999 Fitzhenry & Whiteside Limited
195 Allstate Parkway, Markham, Ontario L3R 4T8

Chapter 1
Death Strikes

As late as 1920, the dreaded, infectious disease, tuberculosis, was still rampant. Doctors knew even less about its cause and cure than they know today about cancer.

Some of the theories in medical books of the day are grimly amusing: "Tuberculosis is due to hereditary disposition, narrow chest, general disease, smallpox, measles, dust or noxious fumes from industrial processes, debauchery, excessive drinking, exposure to cold, and, in the case of women, too-tight corsets."

The suggested cures were no more reassuring. Among those advocated were taking cod liver oil, sweet cream, the juice of a dozen lemons daily, or raw eggs in wine; breathing the purest and driest atmosphere; wearing flannel next to the skin; walking, and salt water bathing.

Perhaps the most enticing cure was a mixture of hops, spikenard root, and the inner and outer portions of tamarack bark, all boiled and drained off to make two quarts of brew, to which was to be added a pound of honey and a pint of the best brandy.

But the disease, also called "consumption" or "phthisis" (wasting away), continued to take its toll.

Sometimes whole families of twelve or more children died during infancy. Cemeteries

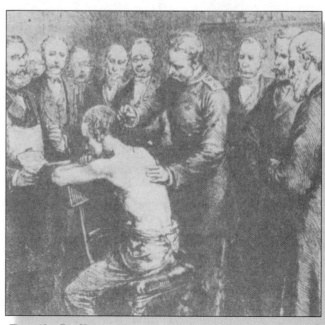

A man suffering from tuberculosis being treated by doctors before a cure had been found for the disease

Alexander Graham Bell when a student in Edinburgh

were full of tombstones denoting this pathetic fact. The disease was thought to be curable, if it was caught in the early stages. Sometimes it did heal on its own (discovered when post mortems revealed scar tissue in the lungs). Occasionally it developed rapidly and was known as "galloping consumption."

It was small wonder, then, that terror struck the hearts of Professor Alexander Melville Bell and his wife, recently arrived in London from Edinburgh, when they learned that their youngest of three sons, Edward Charles, was apparently stricken with the disease.

Edward had never been strong; he had grown too quickly and at the age of eighteen was just under two metres in height. He looked pale and had lost weight, which caused his parents much secret concern. They understood that the disease flourished in crowded cities, and that the atmosphere around their home in Harrington Square was not likely to improve their son's health. Before they fully realized it, Edward had slumped into the advanced stages of the disease. Nothing the doctors could suggest helped. Within the year he was dead.

Alexander Graham Bell was at his brother's bedside when he died. He wrote in his diary, "Edward died this morning at ten minutes to four o'clock. He was only eighteen years, eight months old. He literally 'fell asleep'. He died without consciousness and without pain while he was asleep. So may I die."

Tragedy was not finished with the Bell family. Alexander's elder brother, Melville James, was conducting his father's elocution classes in Edinburgh, when he caught a cold. He could not shake it and the cold soon developed into a nasty, hacking cough. He became pale and feverish. He was depressed, and lacked energy.

By the time Alexander arrived to help relieve his brother of his duties, Melville was losing weight, and blood was mixed with the stringy phlegm which he brought up in spasms of coughing.

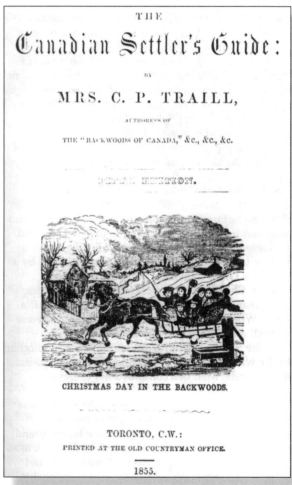

The writing of Catharine Parr Traill provided a vivid picture of life in early Canada for readers overseas ~ a view that enticed many in Britain to emigrate.

THE

Canadian Settler's Guide:

BY

MRS. C. P. TRAILL,

AUTHORESS OF

THE "BACKWOODS OF CANADA," &c., &c., &c.

FIFTH EDITION.

CHRISTMAS DAY IN THE BACKWOODS.

TORONTO, C.W.:
PRINTED AT THE OLD COUNTRYMAN OFFICE.

1855.

Then the doctors became hopeful. Melville appeared to improve and was able to take an interest in his newly arrived son, named Edward Charles Ottoway Bell. Plans for the baby's future were useless, however, as the child died shortly after birth.

Melville James' days were numbered. Few people realized then that often in the advanced stages of tuberculosis the patient appears to be better and the coughing ceases. Melville, who perhaps knew better, took his wife to London, leaving Alexander to carry on his classes in Edinburgh. Alexander never saw his older brother again, for in May, 1870, at the age of 25, Melville died.

When Alexander arrived home, the distraught parents had further cause for alarm. He too had become thin and pale and a telltale flush sometimes appeared on his cheeks. The specialist who examined him gave an unfavourable report. Alexander was dangerously ill.

The family knew they must delay no longer. The situation required drastic action. To save his only surviving son, Professor Bell did not hesitate to give up his rapidly growing classes, his university connections, and his place in the British scientific community. He had spent some time in Newfoundland and remembered its bracing and invigorating climate. He wrote immediately to his friend, the Reverend Thomas Henderson, a retired Baptist minister who lived in Paris, Ontario, to explore the possibilities of immigrating to Canada.

Chapter 2

Family Tree

Before tragedy struck, the Bell family had been happy and eminently successful. There had been three Alexanders in the family, including a grandfather born in St. Andrews. He had wanted to be an actor but at that time in Scotland the theatre was not considered respectable. Consequently, the first Alex did what he considered the next best thing and set himself up as a teacher of speech and elocution. He wrote a textbook called *Elegant Extracts* – it was proper to read the works of Shakespeare, and even to recite them in public, but not to act them on stage. Grandfather Alex also founded a very successful school for boys in Dundee.

Alexander Melville Bell, the father, was born in Edinburgh in 1819. In his early youth he visited Newfoundland and was impressed by the fresh air of the North American continent.

The Bell family's home at 16 Charlotte Street, Edinburgh

Blessed with an abundance of talents, he developed the teaching of speech to a science and wrote a book called *Bell's Standard Elocutionist*, published in 1860. On the public platform the family gift for acting came to the fore and his audiences were enthralled by every word he said.

While in Edinburgh, Alexander Melville decided one

Four generations: Elsie Bell Grosvenor holds her son, Melville Bell Grosvenor. Her father, Alexander Graham, stands between them and Alexander Melville Bell

day to have his portrait painted in miniature by a Miss Eliza Grace Symonds, daughter of a naval surgeon. She was very impressed with this exciting young man about to make a name for himself in the world. When the portrait was finished, the two were married, and settled down in a flat at 16 South Charlotte Street. Bell hung out his signboard indicating that he was a professor of elocution and began to build up a clientele. Mrs. Bell continued her career as a portrait painter.

They had three children, all boys. Alexander was the second, born March 3, 1847. He himself later adopted the name Graham from a close family friend. This third Alexander regarded speech, not as simply the art of elocution, but as a practical means to an end. He possessed many talents, in music, art, and poetry, but beyond these he possessed an insatiable curiosity and an inborn inventiveness and creativity.

His natural interests were science-oriented and showed themselves early in his career. He kept a museum, collected and classified the bones of animals, and observed the stars. His great love was botany.

When he was only eleven, Alexander Graham Bell made his first real discovery. His best friend was a boy of the same age, Ben Herdman, whose father ran a flour mill. Ben had been brought to Professor Bell for speech lessons.

As the mill was just fifteen minutes from Prince's Gardens on the outskirts of Edinburgh, Alex often went there to play with his friend. One day Ben's father caught the boys playing a harmless trick on him.

"You young rascals," he grumbled. Mr. Herdman was too busy to show much patience. "Why don't you make yourselves useful?"

"What could we do?"

"Find a way to remove the husks from this damp grain."

"We'll try," said Alex, "but why don't you simply rub the grains together?"

"There's too much of it, and besides, it won't rub off when it's wet," answered Mr. Herdman.

A century after the birth of Alexander Graham Bell, Canada's Post Office issued a 4-cent commemorative stamp in 1947.

Alex took a handful of the grain home with him to experiment further. He thought a stiff nail brush might do the job and tried it. It worked perfectly, stripping the husks off cleanly.

He raced back to the mill to show his friend Ben and Ben's father.

"Well done, Alex!" declared Mr. Herdman, "But I can't brush all of this." He pointed to the brimming bins of waiting grain.

Alex was not discouraged. A short time later, he came upon an old vat in a forgotten corner of the mill yard. It was lined with wire and in the centre was a paddlewheel which went round and round when the crank was turned. No one seemed to remember what it was for but the sight of it delighted Alex.

"Look here, Ben," cried Alex as he turned the crank.

The grain was squeezed against the wire mesh and the husks came off cleanly.

"You've done it!" shouted Ben excitedly. "Let's go show my dad."

Mr. Herdman was extremely pleased but he didn't say much. He never did. Later, however, when he met the elder Bell, he commented, "Clever lad that Alex of yours, Professor. He'll go far with that kind of inventive mind - mark my words."

Chapter 3
Wonders of Speech

Young Alex continued to experiment. His father had invented "Visible Speech" and Alexander's experiments naturally stemmed from this interest. Visible Speech was a code of symbols which indicated the position and action of the throat, tongue, and lips in uttering various sounds. It was a key to the pronunciation of words in all languages, and it was developed to help guide the deaf in learning to speak. Professor Bell trained his two sons not only to write Visible Speech but also to identify any symbol and repeat the sound it represented. He then gave public demonstrations of his system.

On one such occasion, the boys had successfully identified bird calls, "welcome" in Gaelic, the first line from the *Aeneid* in Latin, and "The Campbells Are Coming," as if played on the bagpipes.

Then came the supreme test. Unknown to Professor Bell, in the audience was a civil servant from India who taught Sanskrit, a basic Indian language.

It was Alex's turn. When he came into the room he saw a symbol which stood for the sound of the letter **t**. Fortunately, he noticed a mark attached which instructed him to use a "soft palate." This was difficult but he managed to do it. The result was a curiously soft sound, as much resembling a **k** as it did a **t**, and quite foreign to the English language.

"Bravo," cried a voice from the audience, as a man rose from his place clapping. "That is absolutely perfect," he announced. It was a unique **t**, found only in Sanskrit, a sound no one else in the assembly had ever heard. The entire audience rose in a standing ovation as Professor Bell, Alex, and his brother bowed deeply in

The words "Visible Speech" written in Visible Speech symbols

acknowledgment.

About the same time, Professor Bell took his sons to see a mechanical man, or *automaton*, developed by Baron von Kempelen many years before. The machine he produced had succeeded where others had failed; it was able to imitate speech, although it spoke in a childish voice. The baron had published a book entitled *The Mechanism of Human Speech* in which he explained the working of the automaton.

Alex was so fascinated that he secured a copy of the baron's book. It was not translated into English and Alex's knowledge of German was not very good. Consequently, he misunderstood the inventor's intention, and this led to a stimulation of his interest and further experimentation along more definite lines.

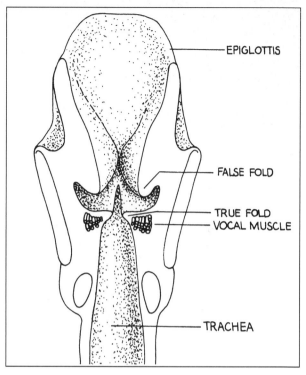

The human larynx

As a result of the visit to see von Kempelen's automaton, Professor Bell encouraged the boys to construct a talking automaton of their own. Alex attempted to build a head while his brother Melville constructed the throat and larynx. The head was made of pliable gutta-percha. Young Alex, who had the fingers of a sculptor, moulded a replica of a human skull, equipped with gums, teeth, and palate. He left holes in the roof of the mouth for nasal passages and in the face for a nose.

The tongue proved to be quite a challenge. It was made of wood in jointed sections and covered with rubber over cotton. It was never entirely satisfactory but it did contribute to the final effect.

Meanwhile, Melville was completing an artificial windpipe of tin, using two tin plates covered with rubber which vibrated by forcing air through the windpipe with organ bellows.

Professor Bell was delighted with their efforts. Alex pleaded excitedly with his father to try the mechanical man.

"All right. Pump air through it, Melville," Professor Bell instructed. To their astonishment, the contraption uttered an unmistakably human "Ah!"

"Try it again," urged Alex as he manipulated the wooden tongue.

This time they were able to produce an equally recognizable "Ma Ma."

As the days went by they became more and more proficient, so much so that they fooled their neighbours, who wondered with some annoyance why the child continued to cry "Mama" without receiving attention!

These lessons left an indelible impression on young Alex and he later tried another experiment. His constant companion was a devoted and obedient Skye terrier. Alex would encourage him to growl continuously and then manipulate his vocal cords. He was able to produce a "ma ma" sound and, by adjusting the dog's tongue, to have it change to "ga ga."

To the delight of the family, he finally had the dog saying, "Ow ah oo ga ma ma." Before long the neighbours were dropping by the house to see the talking dog.

All of these experiments influenced Alexander Graham Bell's destined career as a teacher of deaf mutes. His misinterpretation of Baron von Kempelen's description of his talking automaton also led him to consider seriously the transmission of sound over wires.

It was at this stage of Alex's career that the Bell family pulled up roots. After Melville's death in 1870 they decided to head for the New World. In about a month they had disposed of their possessions, settled their business affairs, and gone through the heart-rending business of saying goodbye to friends and relatives.

Now they were mounting the gangplank to the deck of the S.S. *Nestorian*, an iron steamer of several thousand tons, propelled by two enormous paddlewheels. She could carry hundreds of passengers and was fully booked.

There were four in the Bell party, for at the last minute the young widow of Melville had decided to accompany them. They carried only light suitcases, as their steamer trunks had been stowed below.

Despite the fact that this steamer was modern for its time and considered fast, they were destined for a two-week journey. Passengers, however, were no longer regarded as intruders by the shipping companies, and the saloons and dining rooms on board were as luxurious as those of any hotel. In addition, entertainment was organized for the amusement of the passengers.

Alex Bell, nevertheless, preferred the open deck to the saloons or stateroom, and spent endless days basking in the sun, breathing the fresh salt breeze deeply into his damaged lungs, and watching the seagulls skim over the surface of the waves.

He thought, too, about the vast distance he was travelling and marvelled how a short two years before, in 1868, the S.S. *Great Eastern* had laid the first transatlantic cable tying London to New York by telegraph. Would these same cables one day carry the human voice as well?

This set him to dreaming. He recalled the experiments of the German, Johann Reis, who in 1860 had developed an instrument out of such unlikely components as a hollowed-out bung of a beer barrel, covered with the skin of a German sausage, to which a strip of platinum was attached by a drop of sealing wax. With this crude device, which he called a *telephone*, Reis did succeed in transmitting a tiny distorted kind of music.

Bell also remembered the Englishman Sir Charles Wheatstone, who in 1840 wrote, "I made in 1823 an important discovery that sounds of all kinds can be transmitted perfectly and powerfully through solid wires and reproduced

A model of the S.S. Great Eastern

Major-General James Wolfe, Commander of British expedition against Quebec, 1759

in distant places."

Alex had read, too, about a Frenchman named Claude Chappe who had committed suicide in 1805, because the French Government had not been interested in his scheme for transmitting messages by a speaking tube or mouth trumpet along a series of semaphore towers.

The monotony of the long sea voyage was finally broken as the steamer entered the Gulf of St. Lawrence. A magnificent panorama unfolded before Alex. During the day it took to cross the giant gulf, he passed the mouth of the Saguenay, the Riviere du Loup, the Montmorency Falls, and the Island of Orleans, before the *Nestorian* dropped anchor beneath the looming rock of the fortress of Quebec.

In his mind's eye, Alex scaled the heights with Wolfe to stand on the Plains of Abraham. He was energized by thoughts of a new life in a new world. He dreamed of ways to conquer this magnificent land and become a part of it.

Chapter 4

A New Home

After disembarking at Quebec, the Bell family boarded a train for Montreal. This part of the Intercolonial Railway was complete in 1870 and linked up with the Great Western for the final journey to Paris, Ontario.

"We are now 1,000 miles from the sea," remarked Professor Bell at Montreal, where they changed trains.

"Have we much further to go, Father?" asked Alex, beginning to appreciate the vastness of his new country.

"About another 500 miles, or about another full day's travel."

The house of the Reverend Thomas Henderson, the first general agent for the telephone, which became Canada's first telephone office.

"I don't know if I can stand much more of this juggling and rocking," complained Mrs. Bell.

"I don't mind that so much," said her daughter-in-law, "but it's draughty, and I'm covered with greasy black soot from the engine's smoke stack."

"Quiet, all of you!" commanded Professor Bell. "The country's beautiful and the promise here is worth the inconvenience of the journey. Mr. Henderson says the winters are cold but the air is dry and crisp. And, most important of all, it's healthy and that's why we're here."

"Did Mr. Henderson describe the property he has in mind for us?" asked Mrs. Bell.

"Aye, he said it was situated on a height overlooking the Grand River about two miles outside Brantford and eight miles from Paris."

Alexander Melville Bell and his family in front of the Homestead in the 1870s

A New Home

"What's it called, Father?" asked young Alex.

Professor Bell explained that it was called Tutelo Heights, but that he intended to call it Melville House. With this answer he turned and smiled at Mrs. Bell who nodded her approval.

The Reverend Thomas Henderson was at the station in Paris to greet his tired and rumpled guests when they got down, stiff-legged, from the train. The long journey was almost over. The Bells were put up overnight at the Henderson house and intended to drive out in the morning to their new home at Tutelo Heights, near Brantford.

Early the next day, they set out in their new phaeton for Brantford, following the winding banks of the Grand River in the open-sided carriage.

Joseph Brant

"All this land back for a distance of six miles from the river once belonged to the Six Nations," said Mr. Henderson.

Young Alexander asked who these people were, keenly interested in his new surroundings and their history.

"They were the aboriginals who remained loyal to Britain during the American Revolutionary War," answered Professor Bell.

"Brantford is named after one of their famous chiefs, Joseph Brant," explained Mr. Henderson.

"But I thought you said the house we're going to live in was built in 1857 by a man called Robert Morton, Father."

"It was, but he purchased the land from a man named Stewart, who acquired 1,000 acres when he married one of the Six Nations women."

By this time they were crossing a bridge over an abandoned canal which had once been busy with shipping from the Grand River. They then turned left onto Mount Pleasant Road and began a gentle climb until they turned onto Tutelo Heights Road.

Mr. Henderson pointed out that the narrow and winding road, which followed the lines of the river bluffs, was once a

Chapel of the Mohawks, built 1787

trail used for generations by the aboriginal peoples. "Stewart gradually sold his holdings, and several comfortable houses, including that of Ignatius Cockshutt, were built across the road from the river."

Now their home came into sight. It looked pleasant. Situated well back from the road, it was partially screened by tall trees and bushy shrubs. It was a two-storey building, with white walls and black trim, and included an attractive porch and conservatory.

While the others surveyed the building, Alex scrambled down and headed for the steep banks at the back of the house which overlooked the river. It was a magnificent view and in the distance he could see the smoking stacks of the struggling town of some seven or eight thousand people. Nearer to him was the steeple of the Mohawk chapel, a landmark of a people he was to come to know intimately and love dearly.

"I know I'm going to like this place, Father, and I've found a spot where I can dream and plan, where nobody will ever bother me."

"Good," replied Professor Bell, "I feel much the same as you!"

The Bell family surveyed their new home, exhausted but exhilarated with what seemed a good, new beginning.

Chapter 5

Experiments in Sound

As Alex's health improved rapidly, he spent many hours in his "dreaming place," wondering and planning for his future. He also became more and more restless. One of the projects he undertook was with the Six Nations peoples on the nearby Reserve. He transcribed their hitherto unwritten language into Visible Speech symbols.

Meanwhile, his father had been invited by Miss Sarah Fuller, principal of a school for the deaf in Boston, to show her staff how to use Visible Speech in teaching the deaf to talk. When Professor Bell had finished his course, he was asked to do a second series for other teachers. Unfortunately, because of a previous engagement, he was unable to lecture personally, but he suggested young Alex should give the course in his place.

A class of deaf children and their instructors in Boston, 1871. Bell is at top right; Sarah Fuller is in middle row, second from left.

Despite the professor's recommendation, the committee was reluctant to invite the junior Alexander Bell. He was only twenty-three. After a great deal of discussion, they finally did extend an invitation. Alex readily accepted, since the board of education was offering 500 dollars to pay the lecturer, and he could use the money.

The younger Bell was so successful that he was invited to several other schools, but after six months he was back in Brantford to continue his experiments.

Soon he was restless again, wanting to do something useful. He decided that a return to London would provide

*Gardiner Greene Hubbard,
Bell's sponsor and future
father-in-law*

George Sanders

him with stimulus and useful contacts.

"You can't risk another illness," said his father. "What about your harmonic telegraph?"

"It's stalled for the moment," Alex replied. He considered his father's concerns about the effects on his health of the damp weather in England. "Well, if I can't go back to London, how about Boston?"

"What would you do there?"

"I think I can earn my living there teaching the deaf, and I can experiment at the same time."

Professor Bell accordingly wrote to his friends, and so it was that Alex set up his practice in Boston and other cities in Massachusetts. He was an immediate success. At the Clarke School for the Deaf in Northampton he was able in a few weeks to teach children over 400 English syllables, some of which they had been unable to learn in two or three years under other methods of instruction.

Alexander Graham Bell was a true humanitarian. He disagreed with the opinion commonly held at the time that "nothing can be done for the deaf." And he soon met up with another man who opposed this view, in Gardiner Greene Hubbard, a Boston lawyer. Hubbard's daughter, Mabel, had been left deaf by scarlet fever when she was four years old. Among other responsibilities, Hubbard was serving as president of the Clarke School, and he was also actively involved in Miss Fuller's school in Boston. He and Alex became extremely close friends.

In October, 1872, Bell opened a school of "Vocal Physiology and Mechanics of Speech" in Boston. Here he gave direct instruction to deaf children in order to demonstrate his methods to other teachers. In the following year he was appointed Professor of Vocal Physiology in the School of Oratory at Boston University and transferred his classes there.

His first pupil was a five-year-old child

1901 Aug 29

named Georgie Sanders, whose father was a wealthy merchant. Georgie had been born deaf, and he had never learned to speak. He and Alex hit it off right from the start. The boy progressed splendidly, so Mr. Sanders arranged for Alex to move into his mother's house in Salem, where Georgie could be with him continually.

This had an added advantage for Bell: Georgie's grandmother allowed him to set up his laboratory-workshops in her basement. Alex worked long hours and far into the night on his experiments, but Mrs. Sanders had no idea what he was trying to develop.

As a result of these months with little sleep and overwork, Alex began to ruin his health once more, and his clientele fell off. If it hadn't been for Mr. Sanders' generosity, Alex would have fared badly during the winter of 1873. He was glad,

Alexander Graham Bell "talks" to Helen Keller. Alexander Melville Bell is on her immediate right

therefore, when he was able in the spring to return to his favourite haunts at Tutelo Heights.

Despite the fatigue and setbacks, Alex had established himself firmly in Boston social and medical circles, and his friendship with Hubbard and Sanders was to have a dramatic and lasting effect on his life and career.

Another phase in Alex's life was ending, possibly one of the most satisfying and promising from a personal point of view.

One of Bell's most famous pupils was Helen Keller, who came to him as a child, unable to see, hear, or speak. She was later to say of Alexander Graham Bell that he dedicated his life to the penetration of that "inhuman silence which separates and estranges" and to raising the standards of education for the deaf, to help make people with hearing impairments more easily and fully part of society.

Helen Keller wrote, "Hearing is the deepest, most humanizing sense man possesses, and lonely ones all over the world have been brought into the pleasant ways of mankind because of Dr. Bell's efforts."

The "Gallow's Frame" telephone

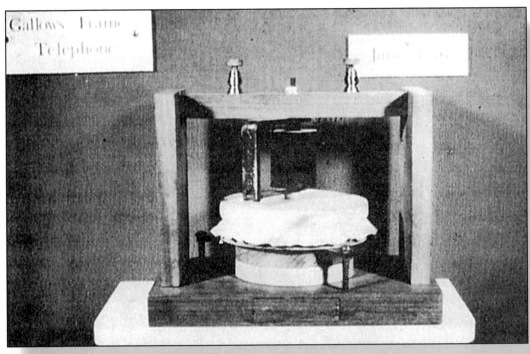

The object of the experiments which Bell was conducting in Boston during the winters of 1873 and 1874 was to send several messages at the same time by what he called his "harmonic telegraph." Sanders and Hubbard thought highly enough of his idea to be willing to support its development with their money. They formed a partnership with the young inventor whereby they would share in any profits as well as the expenses.

Alexander Graham Bell had first become interested in this aspect of the transmission of sound through a book by Hermann von Helmholtz, a German scientist living in London. Helmholtz had managed to produce synthetic vowel sounds by electrically operated tuning forks. Bell misunderstood what he read and thought Helmholtz had sent these sounds from one point to another over a wire. This set Bell once more to thinking about "telegraphing speech."

Bell remembered, too, how Johann Reis had successfully transmitted musical tones over wire by using the "make-and-break" current of telegraphy. Would it be possible, he wondered, by using several tuning forks, to send more than one tone over the same wire simultaneously and then separate the various tones at the receiving end? Bell thought it could be done and began attempting to devise this instrument, which he called a harmonic telegraph.

Bell soon found he lacked the time and skill to make the necessary mechanical parts for his apparatus, so he went for help to the electrical shop of Charles Williams Junior, at 109 Court Street in Boston. The man assigned to help him was Thomas A. Watson.

Thomas Watson was only twenty years of age, largely

without a formal education, but a rapid and accurate workman. The two enthusiastic young men got on well immediately and became firm friends.

Bell's fertile mind was teeming with ideas. He had several plans developing at the same time. One problem he faced was to get several pairs of tuning forks of different pitch to vibrate in resonance with each other, and only with each other, at the same time. He never did quite succeed with this, and decided to switch to steel organ reeds.

Bell reasoned, correctly, that if many reeds of different pitches were vibrating at the same time over an electromagnet, they would generate one complex, varying current. Now, from his experience with music, he knew that if you sing into the sound box of a piano when the dampers are not touching the strings, several strings will sound in sympathy with your voice. If, then, a "harp transmitter" were built with enough strings or reeds, it could pick up every sound of a human voice. The ultimate telephone was one step nearer.

Two things prevented its immediate realization, however. First, Bell's theoretical "harp transmitter" was too complicated to be practical, and secondly his financial backers, who had already invested over $100,000, felt his harmonic telegraph was a more realistic prospect, and promised commercial returns in the more immediate future.

So Bell put aside his ideas for a telephone at this time and concentrated on his harmonic telegraph. Before long, with experiment, patience and diligence, he managed to basically perfect a working model, and demonstrated it to a representative of Western Union over wires from New York to Philadelphia. He ultimately patented his invention in 1875, but not before engaging in a long legal wrangle with a man named Elisha Gray, who claimed to have invented a similar instrument.

The invention could not have reached the public at a better time. There were two rival telegraph companies: Western Union and the Pacific Line. Western Union had enjoyed a monopoly, but the Pacific Telegraph Company bought a patent for $750,000 which allowed it to send four messages at a time along the same wire. The result was that Pacific could reduce prices and at last successfully compete with Western Union.

Bell's invention, which remarkably permitted transmission of up to 30 or 40 messages simultaneously, enabled Western Union to recover lost ground in this early battle of communications giants.

Also in 1875, Bell patented a number of other inventions that emerged from his research. One of these was a form of "autograph telegraph," by which an autograph message or picture might be almost instantly copied in ordinary ink on ordinary paper.

Another Bell invention from this period was the result of his continued interest, only temporarily suspended, in the transmission of the human voice.

Bell had been struck by the dull monotone aspect of the speech of the deaf children he had taught to speak. If only they could learn to *vary* the tone, to show pity, fear, anger, and a thousand other shades of emotion!

This led the relentless inventor to investigate two developments of the same period that he had heard something about.

The first of these was a "monometric capsule," in which a gas flame rose and fell in flickering waves according to the force of the tone of voice.

The other, Bell felt, was more useful. It was called

The human ear

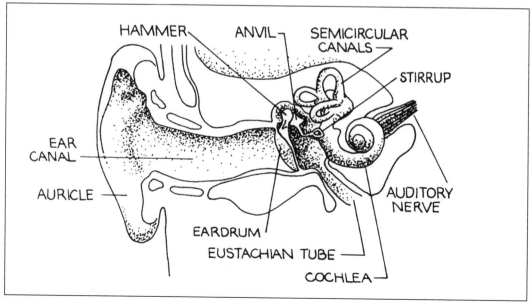

"phonautograph" and consisted of a mouthpiece, a stretched membrane to which a stiff bristle-like brush was attached, and a smoked glass on which the bristle made a pattern when the membrane vibrated to the changes in the intensity of the voice. It is not hard to see how this helped lead to the development of his autograph telegraph.

In using the phonautograph, Bell was struck by its similarity to the membrane and bones of the human ear. It seemed to him that if he could make a receiver which more closely resembled the membrane and the anvil, hammer, and stirrup bones of the human ear, he might get more accurate tracings of voice sounds on the glass.

Consequently, Bell mentioned his idea to a friend, Dr. Clarence J. Blake, an ear specialist.

"Why don't you use a human ear, then?" asked Dr. Blake.

"Where, in heaven's name, could I get a human ear?" exclaimed Bell in astonishment.

"I'll get you one," said Blake and, true to his word, he soon sent one in the mail. The ear arrived with a note explaining that it had come from a corpse at the medical school where Dr. Blake taught.

In the summer of 1874, Alexander Graham Bell returned home for a vacation with his head full of ideas about the telephone. According to his father, he would talk of nothing else.

Chapter 6
First Phones

Alexander Graham Bell relaxed in his favourite hammock behind his home looking out on the wandering Grand. Although his body was at rest, ideas were as usual racing and jostling each other inside his head.

Recalling the human ear which he had substituted as a receiver in the phonautograph, he was struck by the fact that the tissue-paper-thin membrane of the ear could activate the much heavier ear bones and set them vibrating.

He reasoned with his father, "What if I were to substitute a thin iron disc for the membrane and let it act upon a much heavier lever of metal and set it vibrating?"

"I don't know. How would you set it vibrating?"

"By transmitting vibrations of varying intensity along a wire by means of an electric current," Alex explained.

Then he retired once more to his "dreaming place" to work it out bit by bit.

Suddenly, what had been the glimmer of an idea became a blinding flash. As is often the case, the missing link in the chain of invention came in a sudden inspiration by sheer accident.

Bell knew now he must create a current which would carry

An undulating sound current

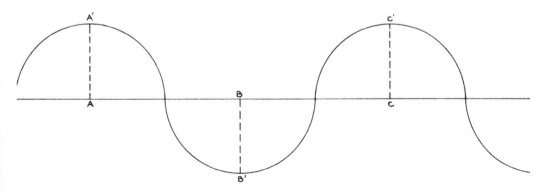

sound waves in the same way that air carries waves from the speaker to the ear of the hearer. It must be a wavy, or undulating, current.

He wrote all these ideas down and discussed them night after night with his father long after the others in the family had gone to bed.

"You see, Father, instead of a multitude of reeds, I'll use a single reed attached to a metal diaphragm, which will vibrate in resonance with the sound produced at the other end and transmitted over a wire by an undulating current."

"It sounds wonderful, but I still don't see it clearly. How will you develop sufficient current to transmit it any distance?"

"I don't quite know yet, Father, but that's a mere detail. I intend to pursue that further when I return to Salem. Perhaps we need very little current. Perhaps the voice itself produces sufficient current."

Later Bell was to write that it was on that July 26, 1874, at Tutelo Heights in Brantford, that the idea of the telephone was first conceived.

Alexander Graham Bell returned to Boston after his vacation in Brantford in that summer of 1874, excited with the idea of a telephone or "electric speech." But he was in a spot.

Over the intervening years Mabel Hubbard, the daughter of one of Bell's backers, had grown into a very attractive young

Mabel Hubbard became Mrs. Alexander Graham Bell

woman, and Alex had fallen deeply in love with her. Fortunately, the feeling was as deep on Mabel's part. They wanted to get married. Mr. Hubbard, however, insisted that Alex become financially self-supporting before he could consent to the marriage. He was disturbed by Alex's apparent inability to complete his work on the harmonic telegraph.

Alex understood that he must be able to support Mabel and could not expect her to scrape along on his meager earnings. He was frustrated, both by the "bugs" in his multiple telegraph equipment and by his ill-concealed desire to pursue his new discoveries related to the telephone. He felt he was very close to a breakthrough and any delay could result in someone else beating him to the punch.

First Phones

Watson sensed this but he said nothing and they continued to experiment, often far into the night.

One day, June 2, 1875, when the two of them were in shirt sleeves because of the oppressive heat, it happened!

Bell was in one room and Watson 20 metres away in another. Bell was tuning one transmitter, which was connected by a wire to another one Watson was adjusting. Suddenly Watson noticed that one of the transmitter springs had ceased to vibrate. He was sure it was stuck so he plucked it loose. At this point Bell came charging in.

"What did you do just now?" he demanded of the startled Watson.

"I just pried loose this jammed spring!"

Alexander Graham Bell and Thomas Watson in the wire-strung laboratory where the first telephone message was transmitted

First Phones

"Don't change a thing! Let me see!"

"This transmitter spring became stuck and I snapped it," Watson repeated, pointing at their contraption.

"I see," said Bell, "and that strip of magnetized steel, by its vibrations over the pole of the magnet, produced the twang I heard so clearly in the other room."

"I don't quite see what you're driving at."

"Don't you see?" asked Alex excitedly. "That strip vibrating produced a current of electricity that varied in intensity in exactly the same way as the air was varying in density within hearing distance of the spring."

Watson laughed excitedly, "You've done it!" He was overwhelmed with the magnitude of the discovery now that he understood.

"I want to be sure. Let's try it again."

Bell and Watson resumed their positions. The spring was plucked again and again throughout the night and each time it produced the same effect. Bell now knew that this undulating current would accomplish what the interrupted current had failed to do. But he had to convince others.

He went to see Mabel's father and explained his new discovery, but Mr. Hubbard remained sceptical and even a little annoyed at this further evidence of Bell's failure to stick to his main purpose, the multiple telegraph.

Alex's heart sank, for he loved Mabel dearly, but he was determined to prove his point. He had to develop a model of his new machine and arouse the interest of someone of influence and understanding.

The next day Bell sat down at his desk and drew up plans for the instrument. He devised a flat wooden plane on which was mounted one of his harmonic receivers, a tightly stretched drumhead parchment, to the centre of which the free end of the receiver was fashioned. He added a mouthpiece, arranged to direct the voice against the other end of the drumhead, which was designed to force the reed to follow the voice vibrations.

Although Watson worked throughout the night, the actual construction was more difficult than drawing the plan. By the following afternoon, however, two instruments were complete and ready for testing.

Watson put one phone upstairs in the attic and ran a wire

down two flights of stairs to his work-bench on the main floor. While Watson listened, Bell shouted and sang into the mouthpiece of his instrument. For a few critical seconds, Bell's heart sank. He heard nothing. Would the brain child live or die?

Then footsteps pounded on the stairs and Watson burst into the room breathless with excitement.

"I could hear you, Alex," he cried. "I could almost make out what you said!"

"We've still got some way to go," Bell responded, elated, "but now we know it will work."

In the next several months Bell and Watson slaved to perfect their precious instrument. Alex was always worried by a shortage of funds and the haunting fear that he would lose his beloved Mabel.

Hon. George Brown

He could not approach Mr. Hubbard again, so in desperation he went once more to Brantford and approached his wealthy neighbour, George Brown, a member of parliament and editor of the Toronto *Globe*, to ask for the sum of $300 to pay his petty debts. Brown greeted him cordially and even agreed to a six-month loan but he insisted on some guarantee, or collateral. Bell agreed to give Brown the British and foreign rights to his invention if Brown would seek a British patent while in England on business. Brown agreed to this as well but, apparently having second thoughts about Bell's "toy," neither secured the patent nor forwarded Alex the loan.

Bell was now desperate; the American patent had also been delayed. Fortunately, at this point Mr. Hubbard became convinced of the worth of his future son-in-law's invention. He was exasperated at Brown's lack of performance. As Alex's legal adviser, he took immediate action and, without even consulting him, filed an application at the Patent Office in Washington. As it turned out, this was not a moment too soon, for Bell's rival, Elisha Gray, filed a provisional patent, or *caveat*, a few hours later the same day!

Chapter 7

Phones Go Far

Dom Pedro II,
Emperor of Brazil

In 1876, three huge battleships lay at anchor in the Schuylkill River of Philadelphia. Naval flotillas were nothing new to the city but these were Brazilian and had brought the Emperor of Brazil, Dom Pedro, to the Centennial Exhibition celebrating the hundredth anniversary of the signing of the Declaration of Independence.

The Centennial Exhibition grounds covered 450 acres along the riverbank including the downtown portion of Fairmount Park. There were two hundred buildings completely packed with all the developments of the previous hundred years.

Alexander Graham Bell did not intend to exhibit his inventions, the multiple telegraph and the telephone. He had all kinds of excuses. They were not yet perfected; his deaf students had examinations coming up soon; finally, the date for entry registration for exhibits had passed.

But another voice was heard, as stubborn as his. Mabel Hubbard had become engaged to Alex on her birthday and she insisted that he exhibit his telephone. This resulted in their first argument, which reportedly involved some hot foot-stamping. Alex finally if reluctantly agreed and Mr. Hubbard found him some space beyond the electrical display in the Massachusetts educational section.

The original model, or "Gallow's Frame" telephone, which they developed in June of 1875, had been improved. On

March 10, 1876 they had tried out a new transmitter in an attempt to produce a stronger undulating current by using a circuit through a galvanic battery. Alex expected he would have to call out as loudly as usual to make himself heard.

"Watson, come here. I want you," he shouted.

Watson came running. "Alex, I heard every word you said – distinctly."

Bell had shouted to his colleague because he had upset acid from a battery onto his clothes, but this announcement by Watson made him forget all about the reason for calling him.

It was this improved model that was on display, but in the six weeks of the exhibition it had drawn little notice. Now it was Sunday, June 25, 1876 and the judges were assessing the exhibits in the electrical area. Bell and Watson had come to Boston to demonstrate the invention if they were presented with an opportunity.

The exhibit judges included Sir William Thomson, later Lord Kelvin, the foremost electrical expert in Britain; Joseph Henry, the American physicist, who had encouraged Bell at an early stage of his work; Professor Barker of the University of Pennsylvania; and Elisha Gray, Bell's keenest rival. Also present was none other than the Emperor Dom Pedro, a guest of the Exhibition Committee.

Sunday had been chosen because visitors from the general public were not admitted that day, but it was hot and sultry and the judges were weary and about to quit. Alex heard them say that they had reached the last exhibit they would look at, and they were still some distance from his telephone. At this moment Dom Pedro spotted Bell and broke away from the others to greet him.

The rest of the party could not understand why the Emperor was paying so much attention to this rather shabbily dressed young man but, out of consideration for their guest, they followed him.

"Mr. Bell, I believe," said the Emperor. "I met you in Boston where you were working with deaf children. I told you I intend to introduce your methods in my country."

"Yes, Your Imperial Majesty."

"What are you doing here?"

"I have a new invention for transmitting speech."

"Well, we must see it!" pronounced Dom Pedro, much to

Bell, the young teacher and inventor, in 1875

the discomfiture of the others in the party who had hoped to escape the heat.

Bell went to the transmitter, leaving Watson to hold the receiver to the Emperor's ear.

"To be or not to be," began Bell, reciting Hamlet's soliloquy.

Dom Pedro almost dropped the receiver as he exclaimed, "My God, it speaks!"

One by one, the members of the party took turns as Bell continued in his best dictation ending with, "And enterprises of great pith and moment/With this regard their currents turn away." Sir William and Lady Thomson were so delighted they took turns listening and speaking, like excited children.

"It's the greatest thing I've seen in America," declared Sir William.

The entire panel was suitably impressed with Bell's invention. When things settled down, the committee gave Alexander Graham Bell the Centennial Award.

Two weeks later Bell returned to Brantford to enjoy a well-earned rest and to share his triumph with his parents. He was still not satisfied, however, as he wished to demonstrate the telephone's capabilities over a long distance.

At home Alex showed that the revamped model worked between an upstairs room and an arbour in the grounds. The neighbours were impressed but Bell planned a much more serious experiment.

This test involved a sound transmission between his home and the village of Mount Pleasant, three kilometres down the road. The receiver was located in a general store kept by Wallis Ellis which also served as an office for the Dominion

Telegraph Company.

There was, however, no line between Tutelo Heights and the main line, so Alex bought all the stove wire available and strung it along the fence posts with the help of his neighbours. One boy even crawled through a culvert taking the wire with him.

Quite a crowd gathered in Ellis' store that evening and they were not disappointed. First they heard Alex's uncle, David Bell, recite another Shakespeare soliloquy, then several solos by local singers. Although listening required considerable concentration, the songs were readily identified. Bell and all concerned were more pleased than at any point in the phone's development.

The ultimate test came several days later, on August 10, 1876. Alex applied to the Dominion Telegraph to use their line between Brantford and Paris, Ontario. Thomas Swinyard, general manager of the telegraph company, regarded the experiment as the work of a crank, and was ready to refuse. His young assistant, Lewis B. McFarlane, rescued Bell's application from the wastepaper basket, and persuaded Swinyard to permit Alex to use the company's lines on the evening of August 10.

Paris was over ten kilometres from Brantford and ideal for the final test. Even so, there were several problems, as the message had to travel all the way to Toronto and then back to Paris, a total distance of 90 kilometres. Bell had reason to be concerned about the success of this venture.

He drove his horse and buggy over to Paris, carrying his equipment in his lap. George Dunlop, the Paris telegraph operator, was alone in the office which occupied part of a boot and shoe store operated by Robert White on Grand River Street. He had met Bell before and they shook hands.

"Do you know the arrangements?" asked Alex.

"Yes. The word's all over town. Everyone's excited and there'll be plenty of townsfolk down here later to witness the test."

The Reverend Thomas Henderson was the first to arrive. He was nervous because he knew how much depended on the success of the test. He was soon joined by Mayor Whitlaw, John Penman, Mr. Clay, Mr. McCash, and other important people of the town. Needless to say, Mr. White, the store

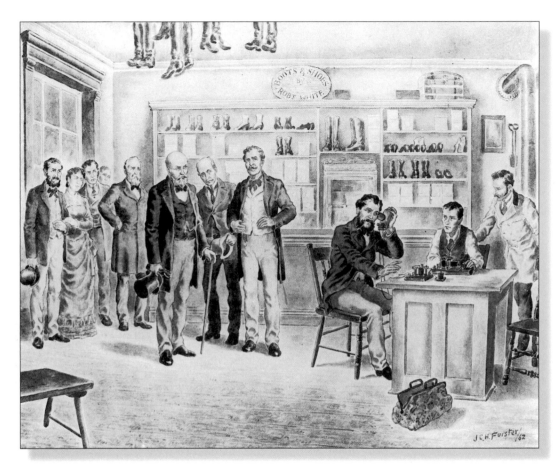

Testing the telephone in Robert White's store

owner, became more concerned as the crowd of dignitaries grew. Finally Dunlop bolted the front door as the shop would hold no more.

When the test began, Bell was worried by the massive interference on the line, which sounded like distant gunfire. He could hear the tune of "The Maple Leaf Forever" but the words were indistinguishable.

"Telegraph them and ask them to adjust the electromagnet coils from low to high resistance," he told Dunlop.

This done, the voice of his uncle reciting from Shakespeare's *Macbeth* came through loudly and clearly. Then David Bell asked, "Can you hear me now?"

"Wire them – yes, I hear you," said Alex.

Then, to Bell's surprise, he thought he heard his father's voice reciting Hamlet's familiar soliloquy; he was surprised because he thought his father had been unable to attend on account of an engagement somewhere else.

"Wire them and ask if that was my father reading," said Alex.

After a slight pause the voice replied, "Yes, my son, this is your father speaking." He went on to explain that he could not stay away and had postponed his appointment in Hamilton in order to be present.

The test was an obvious success. The telephone was no longer a toy, but the first two-way conversation was still to come. This took place between Cambridgeport and Boston on October 9, 1876.

The year 1876 had gone well but 1877 went even better. In July of that year Alexander Graham Bell married Mabel Hubbard and sailed with her to England.

He introduced the telephone to Britain and demonstrated it to Queen Victoria. The Queen wrote in her journal, "A Professor Bell explained the whole process, which is not extraordinary." On the whole, however, his efforts in England were disappointing. A rival company infringed on his patents, and captured most of the business.

In 1878, the Bells returned to the United States and moved to Washington, D.C. Alex took little part in the telephone business except to defend his patents in law suits, some of which reached the Supreme Court. In every one, the court upheld Bell's rights.

Bell now turned his interests to new fields. In 1880 he was awarded the Volta Prize of 50,000 francs for his invention of the telephone and promptly used the money to establish the Volta Laboratory in Washington.

Queen Victoria

Boston Insurance Company John Hancock recognized Bell's importance in this 50s magazine ad.

He made a magic wire talk your language…

The monophone used by King George VI and Queen Elizabeth on their visit to Canada in 1939

Bottom left: Telephone made between 1908 and 1912

Bottom right: Edmonton's first dial phone

Phones Go Far

Chapter 8
Other Phones

At the Volta Laboratories, Alexander Graham Bell had two associates: Summer Tainter, an optical instrument-maker, and his cousin Chichester Bell.

Alex and Tainter turned their attention to experimenting with the element named *selenium*. This element changes its resistance to electricity when it is exposed to light. It then produces an undulating light beam which functions through the atmosphere as the undulating current functioned over a wire. Thus Bell was able to transmit sounds, over short distances, on a beam of light.

Bell wrote enthusiastically, "I have heard a ray of the sun laugh, cough, and sing."

He called the device the *photophone*, but a French scientist, Ernest Mercadier, pointed out that as Bell used radiant energy it should more accurately be called a *radiophone*. This was probably the first invention to which the prefix "radio" was applied. Although Bell was convinced that the radiophone was practical, it was never fully developed during his lifetime.

Inventor Thomas Alva Edison

Bell and Tainter concentrated on a new invention that some others had dropped as a mere toy, or as being quite impractical.

Thomas Edison had been working on a talking machine which he called the *phonograph*. Edison may not have been the first man to be struck with the idea. A French poet and

The original tin-foil phonograph

amateur scientist, Charles Cros, had deposited a sealed paper with the Academie des Sciences on April 30, 1877, because he had not been able to raise sufficient money to pay for a patent. In this paper he described the process of obtaining tracings of sound waves on a lampblocked glass disc and photoengraving the tracings into reliefs or indentations.

Edison's invention had some differences, in that he used a cylinder instead of a disc, and embossed or indented the recorded material on tin foil with a flexed needle, or *stylus*. Furthermore, Edison not only described it but built a working model. Edison obtained a patent on February 19, 1878.

But Edison's phonograph was imperfect in many ways. It could record only for two minutes at the most, and the sound was distorted and indistinct. The recording also wore out after two or three playings. Edison, after producing five hundred examples of the new device as a novelty toy for public exhibitions, abandoned the phonograph to concentrate on producing an incandescent electric light.

The Volta Laboratories had already patented devices for the transmission and recording of sound by gaseous or liquid jets and by radiant energy. They now took on the project of perfecting Edison's phonograph.

They made several refinements. In place of Edison's tin foil, they substituted a cardboard cylinder coated with wax, in which the recording stylus engraved the patterns of its vibrations in narrow grooves. And in place of Edison's rigid needle, they developed a loosely mounted stylus. Finally they achieved a steadier and constant speed for recording and reproducing sound by using a foot treadle, and later an electric motor, instead of Edison's hand crank. This did away with the weird fluctuations in pitch that plagued Edison's machine. Bell and Tainter received a patent for their machine, which they called the *graphophone*, on May 4, 1886.

Before introducing the graphophone to the public, Bell and Tainter informed Edison of their developments and suggested he might like to cooperate in perfecting and marketing it. Edison scorned their offer and threatened to run them out of the market.

Edison then proceeded to produce a machine with a wax cylinder and a floating stylus, which bore a striking resemblance to the Bell-Tainter graphophone. Bell and Tainter, meanwhile, had sold production rights to the American Graphophone Company, which came into being in June, 1887. The company lost their advantage, however, by attempting to sell it chiefly as a dictaphone, for business use.

The American Graphophone Company prepared itself to be sued by Edison, but he never brought an action, because his original patent specifically mentioned "embossing

An Edison Spring-Motor phonograph, 1895

A photograph of Edison taken at 5:30 a.m. on June 16, 1888, after he had worked all night on an improved phonograph

and indenting," while the Bell-Tainter patent described the process as "engraving."

The matter was finally solved when in 1888, Jesse H. Lippincott, a businessman from Pittsburgh, bought the sole rights to American Graphophone for $200,000, and then secured Edison's patent rights for half a million. Edison was free to manufacture, and for this purpose a single company, known as the North American Phonograph Company, was incorporated on July 14, 1888.

Bell, in typical fashion, contributed his full share of the $200,000 from the sale to found the Volta Bureau for research to aid the deaf, which still exists in Washington, D.C., carrying on this valuable and humanitarian work.

Chapter 9
Sallies into Medicine

Alexander Graham Bell and Mabel Hubbard Bell were not spending all their time in Washington during these years. It is true that Bell's father had been persuaded to move to Washington in 1881, but Alex was looking about for a summer home elsewhere.

The Bells and their two little girls, Elsie May and Marion (Daisy), first saw Cape Breton Island and Baddeck in Nova Scotia in the summer of 1885. (The Bells' two sons had died in infancy.)

Mrs. Bell's mother had first aroused their interest in Nova Scotia when she described the fir and spruce trees there as the finest she had ever seen. They travelled the Bras d'Or lake on the old steamer *Marion*, and were so delighted with the beautiful countryside, which reminded Alex of Scotland, that they decided to return the following summer and "build a little cabin beside some

The Hall and Point, Beinn Bhreagh, 1908

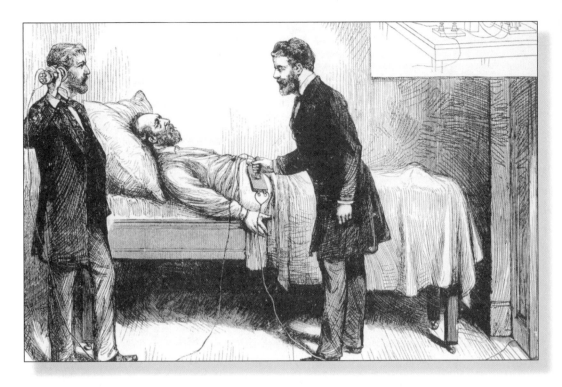

Using a telephone and induction coil, Bell and Tainter attempted to locate the bullet lodged near President Garfield's spine.

running brook."

They returned in 1886 but found no running brook. So they rented a small cottage at Crescent Grove on Baddeck Bay, a couple of kilometres out of town.

Across Baddeck Bay was a massive headland called Red Point, which they climbed while exploring one day. On the peak they were amazed to see the magnificent panorama of lakes and hills. At this instant they determined to buy the whole hill.

Negotiations for land took time, and it was not until 1890 that the last tract was acquired. Bell, however, would not build until he was sure of an adequate water supply. At last, one of the properties was found to contain a spring and with this secure a permanent home was built in 1892. The estate was named *Beinn Bhreagh*, Gaelic for "beautiful mountain." The original "little cabin" became a lodge of thirteen rooms with a beautiful garden and farm attached.

It was on this farm that Alex made one of his first forays into medicine. He became interested in the scientific breeding of sheep, trying to develop a ewe that would bear several lambs at a time, instead of the usual one.

In the field of eugenics, Alexander Graham Bell published a massive book entitled *Duration of Life and Conditions Associated with Longevity*. In this exhaustive study Bell obtained statistics on 8,907 members of the Hyde family. Tracing it back to a common ancestor, he made a scientific study of its genetic development.

Another opportunity for Alex to prove his ingenuity and skill occurred after an attack on US President James Garfield, on July 2, 1881.

Garfield was shot in the back as he walked through the Washington railway station. Surgeons were unable to locate the bullet in crudely probing the wounded president. Bell developed experimental electronic and exploratory devices that might have helped save Garfield's life, had they been applied early and properly, but Garfield's condition deteriorated over the hot summer and, despite heroic efforts to save him from the assassin's bullet, he died September 19.

Dr. and Mrs. Alexander Graham Bell, with their daughters Elsie and Daisy, in 1885

Still, Bell's inventions continued to be used for similar medical procedures until superseded by the X-ray.

Alexander Graham Bell was also ahead of his time when he proposed the use of a radium capsule in the treatment of deep-seated cancer. In July of 1903 Alex wrote to his friend, Dr. Sowers of Washington, and suggested that the reason radium was not successful in these cases was because of the amount of the healthy tissue between the capsule and the tumour. "There is not reason, however," he said, "why a tiny fragment of radium sealed up in a fine glass tube should not be inserted into the very heart of the cancer." While Bell did not claim to have originated this idea, the use of radium in the way he described eventually became widespread.

Finally, Alex outlined yet another aid to medicine in an 1882 article entitled, "A Proposed Method of Producing Artificial Respiration by Means of a Vacuum Jacket." In it he described the principles essential in the modern "iron lung," many years before it came into regular use.

These were busy years for Alex and his family, as he shuttled back and forth between Washington and Baddeck, his mind always filled with new ideas in many different fields.

Chapter 10
Into The Air

Alexander Graham Bell was possessed with an insatiable scientific curiosity and driving energy. At an early date he became interested in flying.

"Write this down, please Watson," directed Bell on June 5, 1892. "The flying machine of the future, as I now conceive it, will be heavier than air and capable of vertical take-off and hovering as well as horizontal flight."

"Did you say 'hover'?"

"I did. I mean somewhat like a hawk."

"How would you achieve that?"

"With jets propelled by burning alcohol on the horizontal blades of a propeller."

"Oh, you mean like that model you called a helicopter, which you built last year?"

"Precisely."

Bell realized many inventors had died trying to fly their experimental aircraft. He realized that the heavier the machine, the greater the speed required to get and keep it aloft. He reasoned, therefore, that he should begin with a machine light enough to be flown as a kite. It was also obvious that equilibrium was a problem and could most safely be studied by flying kites. Finally, he believed

Strange wheels float like feathers above a field at Beinn Bhreagh

landing and takeoff were the greatest hazards and would be minimized by operating from water.

Bell's flying kites amused the villagers, who tolerated his eccentricities. This comment of a boatman was typical: "He goes up there on the side of the hill on sunny afternoons with a lot of thingamajigs, and fools away the whole blessed day, flying kites, mind you. He sets up a blackboard, and puts down figures about these kites and queer machines he keeps bobbing around in the sky. He has dozens of them, all kinds of queer shapes, and the kites are but poor things, God knows! I could make better myself. And the men that visit him – grown men – that should have something better to do. They go up there with him and spend the whole

Multiple triangular-cell kite, 1902

"Siamese Twin" kite, 1905

Into The Air

livelong day flying kites. It's the greatest foolishness I ever did see."

From his kite experiments, particularly with Hargrave box kites, Bell realized that several similar structures, or "cells," packed tightly together would overcome the problem of the weight of the machine by increasing the surfaces for the required lift. Bell replaced the easily distorted rectangular cell of Laurence Hargrave, an Australian, with a strong, rigid triangular prism or *pentahedral* cell, and eventually, two triangular bird-like wings at a *dihedral* (two surfaces meeting) angle of about 70 degrees. Bell not only experimented with this form in kites but used it as sails on boats, and found he could tack exactly as with ordinary sails.

By 1903, Bell had developed *Mabel II*. This flying construction consisted of a bank of sixteen cells more than ten metres wide. To launch it, the kite was mounted on three parallel floats built to *tetrahedral* cell frames covered with oilcloth. It was towed by a steamboat at twelve to thirteen knots in a heavy downpour. The kite carried an estimated thirty kilograms of absorbed water. It had remarkable stability in squalls but still lacked lift. As Bell considered stability to be essential, since the kite was to be responsible for human lives, he refused to sacrifice steadiness to increase the lift.

After 1903, aluminum tubing replaced the frames of black

The Bells strolling in the garden at Beinn Bhreagh

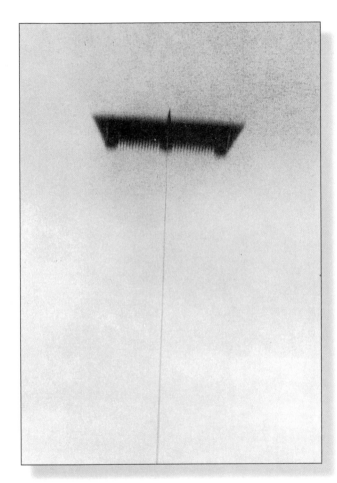

Cygnet, 1907

spruce, and in 1904 Bell added a tail in tandem to improve the longitudinal stability of the tetrahedral kite. Finally, in 1905, he developed a kite which lifted 75-kilogram Neil McDermid ten metres into the air.

The ultimate man-carrying kite was completed on November 13, 1907 and was christened *Cygnet*. Towed by a steamer, it was launched December 3, 1907 and flew steadily. The wind speed at takeoff was nearly 50 km/hr; the elevation 26 degrees 30 minutes; and the pull exceeded the capacity of the balance, about 90 kilograms.

Three days later, Lieutenant Thomas E. Selfridge, of the newly formed Aerial Experiment Association, flew aboard the *Cygnet*, ascending to a height of sixty metres. Then

The "Wheel Kite." The boy is Melville Bell Grosvenor, Dr. Bell's grandson

the wind dropped and the machine began to descend after about seven minutes in the air.

The Aerial Experiment Association was founded at Hammondsport on Lake Keuka in September of 1907. The Association was Mrs. Alexander Graham Bell's idea, and she provided the necessary funds. Other members were Dr. Bell, Glenn Curtiss, Frederick Walker ("Casey") Baldwin, Lieutenant Thomas Selfridge, and later John A.D. McCurdy.

Glenn Curtiss was the young founder of the G.H. Curtiss Manufacturing Company of Hammondsport, New York. He had begun as a manufacturer of motorcycles but switched to building motors for lighter-than-air craft. His sister became deaf and the family moved to Rochester so that she could attend a school for the deaf in the town. On a visit there, Dr. Bell sought out Curtiss and described his kite experiments and his plan to install a motor in a kite capable of carrying a person. He caught the imagination of Curtiss, who became the chief rival of the Wright brothers in developing power flight in America.

"Casey" Baldwin was of Irish descent. His great-grandfather, Dr. William Warren Baldwin, left Cork, Ireland, and settled in Durham on the north shore of Lake Ontario. He later moved to York (Toronto), and forsook medicine for law. His son, Robert, joined his father in a law partnership. They entered politics and played a leading role in the struggle for responsible government in Canada following the Act of Union in 1841. Robert was the Baldwin of the two Baldwin-Lafontaine ministries of 1842-43 and 1848-51. One of Robert's grandchildren was Frederick Walker Baldwin, born in Toronto on January 2, 1882.

F.W. Baldwin began his secondary education in 1893 at Ridley College, St. Catharines. There he was nicknamed "Casey", after the hero of the poem "Casey at the Bat." This was appropriate, because of his Irish ancestry and skill in sports. He graduated from the School of Practical Science (SPS) with a diploma in Mechanical-Electrical Engineering in 1906.

F. W. (Casey) Baldwin (1908)

May 18 '08

Members of the Aerial Experiment Association left to right: Mr. Glenn W. Curtiss, Dr. Bell, Mr. J.A.D. McCurdy, Mr. F.W. Baldwin

John Alexander Douglas McCurdy was born in Baddeck, Nova Scotia. His father, A.D. McCurdy, was the editor of the local newspaper, and his grandfather had been a member of the Legislative Council of Nova Scotia. Shortly after the arrival of the Bells in Baddeck, he was persuaded to become Alexander's secretary.

McCurdy and Baldwin had attended the SPS at the same time and were close friends. McCurdy told Baldwin of Bell's experiments and invited him to visit Baddeck. Baldwin, who was excited by the idea of mechanical flight, readily accepted the invitation.

Lieutenant Thomas Etholen Selfridge was a young artillery officer in the United States Army. He was convinced of the practicality of mechanical flight and that aircraft would prove to be an important part of the weaponry of future warfare. Born in California and having studied aviation, Selfridge wished to gain practical experience. He visited Dr. Bell in Washington and was persuaded to come to Baddeck to see Bell's kite experiments.

Thus each member brought his individual skills and interests to the association. In all, they were to produce four pusher-biplanes in 1908-9, called *aerodromes*. (The term has over the course of the century come to mean, not airplanes, but places where airplanes take off and land.)

One of the first projects of the Aerial Experiment

Association was the completion of Alexander Graham Bell's tetrahedral-cell aerodrome. Dr. Bell assigned Curtiss the job of producing a 16-horsepower motor weighing under 50 kilograms. In the interval, he himself resumed work on aerial propellers. He made several models of various diameters and pitch, including one of variable pitch.

For testing his propellers, Bell built a large catamaran which he called the "Ugly Duckling."

"Well, here's your engine, Dr. Bell," announced Curtiss.

"What is its horsepower and what does it weigh?"

"It develops 20 horsepower and weighs 55 kilograms."

"It sounds good! We'll give it a try."

The engine, however, was damaged in shipping. Bell then ordered a larger one, on condition that Curtiss deliver it in person and explain how it worked. Alex offered to pay him $25 a day for his trouble. Curtiss accepted and, under the spell of Bell and his associates, stayed to become their engine expert.

When it was decided to build a rigid biplane capable of supporting an engine and a passenger, they came face to face with the real problem – stability and control in the air. Up until then, planes could operate only if there was little or no wind. Lateral balance was restored by the use of the rudder, and the machine was turned into the wind to increase the lift. Response was slow. In turns, balance was destroyed for the same reason and the resulting tilt and sideslip were only counteracted, and then inadequately, by the vertical fin area, or

"Oionos I" on the ice, 25 March 1910

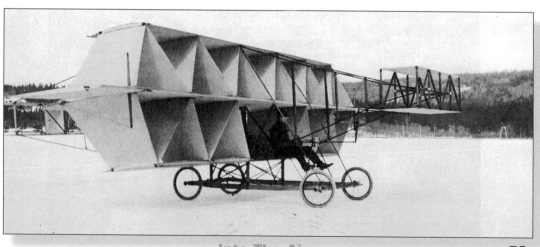

Red Wing: *1908*

by the aviator's shifting his body.

The Aerial Experiment Association achieved a measure of longitudinal stability by the "longitudinal dehedral," a large, fixed tail surface three metres aft of the wings, and by using a wing section of curvature. Vertical control was provided by a "bow" control (elevator), a pivoted flat surface two metres ahead of the wings. Horizontal control was provided by a vertical rudder pivoted at the leading edge, at the centre and above the rear tail surface.

Because this Drome Number 1 was covered with red silk it was christened *Red Wing*. It was driven by a Curtiss eight-cylinder air-cooled V-motor weighing 68 kilograms and at flying speed rated 1,200 r.p.m. and 25 h.p.

On March 12, 1908, Casey Baldwin took off in the *Red Wing*. After a run of about 50 metres on the ice of Lake Keuka, the craft lifted, slowly climbed, and flew steadily at an estimated height of four metres. This continued for some 100 metres, before the buckling of a strut of the tail surface forced the craft roughly down. The flight, made on the first attempt, measured 97 metres, the longest first flight of any such machine. Thus Baldwin not only made the first public flight in a heavier-than-air machine in North America, but was the first Canadian to fly any heavier-than-air craft.

After the crash of the *Red Wing*, Bell suggested a number of improvements to ensure lateral stability. He suggested movable surfaces at the wing tips, operated by the instinctive movement of the aviator through a shoulder fork. On the *Red Wing*, the triangular tips of the upper wing, if hinged and operated differentially, would have provided lateral control and might also have assisted in turns. Dr. Bell thus independently suggested the *aileron*, which had already been used by Pelterie and Bleriot.

Work began at once on the *White Wing*, which was covered with white cotton. It incorporated "lateral rudders" and ailerons, or hinged wing tips. This was a first for North American planes. The *White Wing* also had the first three-wheeled undercarriage and the engine was controlled by a foot throttle.

The first trial of the *White Wing* was made on May 14, 1908 by Lieutenant Selfridge from the local racetrack at Hammondsport. Selfridge reported that the rudder was inadequate for ground control but the front wheel, fitted with fork and tiller, proved satisfactory.

On May 18, Casey Baldwin made a short flight of 85 metres, again at a height of about four metres. Next day Selfridge made two flights of about 30 metres, barely above ground surface, then an encouraging flight at a height of six metres that covered over 70 metres.

Curtiss then hopped in for a fourth flight. This covered 300 metres, at a speed of over 50 km/hr. McCurdy made the fifth flight, but the wing tip struck the ground and the plane flipped over. Neither McCurdy nor the engine was injured but the fuselage was extensively damaged. It was decided to salvage what was of use and start construction of the AEA's third machine.

The plane, dubbed *June Bug*, included certain modifications in the ailerons, and the pilot's seat was positioned to permit aileron-operating gear to be simplified.

White Wing: *1908*

On June 19, Curtiss made three successive flights of 140, 125 and a startling 385 metres. Things were really beginning to get exciting. The next morning, another flight of 660 metres was made in 41 seconds. The same evening, after a larger elevator and rudder were fitted, Curtiss flew an amazing 1,040 metres in 60 seconds, achieving an air speed of approximately 60 km/hr.

The day after this flight Dr. Bell wired his patent attorneys to examine the *June Bug* for patentable features. No further flights were to be made until after that examination.

On July 20, 1908 Orville Wright served notice that the "lateral rudders" infringed on a broad Wright patent, which resulted in lengthy law suits. Bell, who remembered his legal troubles over the telephone, was convinced that "our invention is not covered by the Wright patent."

Despite the Wright patent, the Aerial Experiment Association was granted a United States patent on December 5, 1911, described as follows: "In a flying machine...a pair of lateral balancing rudders, one on each side of the medial fore and aft line of the structure, and each normally having a zero angle of incidence, and connections between said rudders whereby one is adjusted to a positive and the other to a

June Bug, *1908*

Into The Air

negative incidence."

The fourth AEA machine incorporated improvements. At McCurdy's insistence, Curtiss designed an eight-cylinder V-engine which was water cooled and developed 50 h.p. at 1,600 r.p.m. It weighed 80 kilograms.

McCurdy pilots his Silver Dart *over Baddeck Bay in the first airplane flight in the British Commonwealth, February, 1909*

The wings were covered with non-porous cloth and the ailerons were enlarged to make turning easier. The covering cloth was silver. The craft was named the *Silver Dart*.

McCurdy flew her on August 27 with one biplane tail surface removed, and then both, and she proved faster and more sensitive. McCurdy flew a three-kilometre, figure-eight course in three minutes and Curtiss, two days later, did the same distance in two minutes twenty-eight seconds.

On September 17, 1908 Lieutenant Selfridge died while testing a plane with Orville Wright in army tests at Fort Myers, Virginia. A month after his death, the association moved back to Baddeck, and McCurdy was elected secretary in Selfridge's place.

Research at the Association benefited from Wright's disaster. Bell concluded that two side-by-side propellers were to be avoided and that all controls should be in front of the aviator. The centre of balance, too, ought to be further back, to prevent stalls and nosedives at low-flight speeds.

McCurdy now suggested they should fit floats on the *June Bug* to see if the air lift was enough to overcome the drag and take her off. After several runs of about a kilometre and a half, at an average speed of 40 km/hr, McCurdy was unable to get her off the ground.

Bell concluded that the flat bottoms on the pontoons created too much suction to permit the takeoff. The men tried foils to lift the pontoons out of the water but could attain a speed of only 12-15 km/hr. Although this machine, called the *Loon*, was unsuccessful, further experimentation was to take place in a related direction.

Chapter 11
Onto The Water

Dr. Bell with his still to provide shipwrecked sailors with fresh water distilled from the sea

In 1909, Baldwin and McCurdy formed the Canadian Aerodrome Company to produce aerodromes of the *Silver Dart* type on a commercial basis, and produced *Baddeck I* and *II*, *Cygnet I* and *II* and *Oionos I*. Meanwhile, the Bell Laboratory returned to some of Alexander's earlier interests.

Ever since he had crossed the Atlantic, Alex had been interested in locating icebergs by a type of echo-sounding equipment. This anticipated the invention of sonar.

He also experimented with the distillation of salt water to provide shipwrecked sailors with a supply of the fresh water necessary for survival.

Bell's greatest marine experiment evolved from his problems with pontoons and his attempts at lifting aircraft off a water surface without the necessity of towing. Beginning in 1911, Dr. Bell returned to his old idea of "studying aviation in a bath tub." Measurements were made more easily on stationary models and the results were applicable to both hydroplanes and aeroplanes.

As part of his experiment, the Bell Laboratory began to work on floats for hulls. When they tried skis, the hull turned turtle. Similar results were obtained with triple sets of "hydrosurfaces" arranged parallel and horizontally. When they substituted five-blade surfaces at a dihedral of 120 degrees, however, the model when towed was perfectly stable even in rough waters. Further experiments proved a 90-degree dihedral was even more suitable. Bell tried applying these hydrosurfaces to sailing vessels with mixed success.

When the United States entered the war in 1917, Bell

returned to his efforts to develop a hydrodrome which would be effective against mines and submarines and also capable of carrying torpedoes.

Casey Baldwin thought the best type of craft for high speed was one with a cigar-shaped hull.

"You mean a dirigible of the ocean," observed Bell.

"Yes, just big enough to float the engines."

HD-4, *October 1919.*
Stern view, showing the slight dihedral angle of the main sets

"It could pass over mine fields, enter harbours, and cause great damage."

"What about its military load?"

"The hydrosurfaces can support enormous loads, as much as ten tons per centare."

The first of these, *HD-1*, had been completed in November of 1911. This was a very short, flat-bottomed boat, two metres in the beam and about four metres long. The hull held the cockpit and one Gnome rotary engine driving a three-metre-diameter, four-blade pusher-propeller. Carried on lateral outriggers from the hull were two sets of cambered horizontal hydrocurves of 30-centimetre span, three metres apart.

On first trials the *HD-1* reached speeds of 45 km/hr. The second trial, on December 7, 1911, upped the speed to 65 km/hr, and by July 16, 1912 she travelled at nearly 75 km/hr.

The *HD-3* removed some of the previous snags but the *HD-4* was by far the best. This craft was carried on three sets of reefing hydrofoils, with aerial propulsion provided by two 250-h.p., 12-cylinder Renault engines. Because of delay in their delivery, she was not launched until October, 1918.

The *HD-4* was designed with a long cigar-shaped hull providing the flotation function, as well as accommodation for the

crew, fuel, and military load. Two cantilever outriggers near the bow carried balancing hulls, the engines on pedestals, and two sets of hydrofoils below. In the hull, between the outrig-

The Bell-Baldwin hydrofoil HD-4 roars across Baddeck Bay at 114 kilometres an hour, September 9, 1919

gers, was a cockpit. Under the aft end, a third set of hydrofoils pivoted to serve as rudder, and under the bow, a "preventer" set of hydrofoils was arranged to prevent diving during takeoff, but which afterwards remained inactive.

The unique hull was intended to provide strength in binding the *torsion* (twisting action). It was cylindrical, twenty metres long, with a maximum diameter of under two metres and tapered toward both ends. This hull was built around six wooden bulkheads with seven fore-and-aft stringers. The skin was canvas laid spirally in marine glue. The outrigger hulls were of similar construction, six metres long and sixty centimetres in diameter, six metres apart and 30 centimetres below the centre of the main hull.

The weight with three men aboard was over 5 tons. Eighty-five various tests with different blade incidence were run and on December 21, 1918 a speed of 85 km/hr was achieved.

As a result of a report submitted to the navy, the Renault engines were replaced by two 12-cylinder, low-compression, water-cooled Navy Type Liberty engines developing 350 h.p. at a weight of nearly half a ton.

With these new engines, during a trial on September 9, 1919, the *HD-4* ran at a speed of 114 km/hr over a kilometre-and-a-half course on quiet water, faster than any previous water craft. The achievement attracted wide interest. Both the United States Navy and the British Admiralty were interested. Applications for patents were filed by Bell in Washington on May 7, 1920, and in London on April 18, 1921.

The Admiralty sent Commander C.C. Dobson, V.C., D.S.O., a former submarine commander and commander of a flotilla which had penetrated the harbour of the Russian port of Kronstadt and had sunk a number of battleships; Engineer Commander W.S. Mann, an expert on engines, and Assistant Constructor G.H. Child, experienced in the design of small craft. They gave *HD-4* nine separate trials between July 7 and 31, 1920.

Dr. Bell and Casey Baldwin in the cockpit of their speedboat

It was not until September 8 of that year that four United States officers arrived to test and inspect. They were Rear-Admiral W. Strother-Smith, Commanders Hepburn and Richardson, and Lieutenant Stott. Despite favourable reports from both groups of examiners, "the operation was successful but the patient died."

During the winter of 1919-20, blueprints had been made for the *HD-5*, a larger and more powerful craft, designed to carry three Lewis guns, as well as two 45-cm torpedoes. Models of the *HD-5* went to the Admiralty for testing in September, 1921. They, too, were approved, but there the matter rested.

Some brief interest was shown in *HD-4* as a tow target, and Dr. Bell offered her for this purpose but the offer was refused. She was beached, and for decades remained as a relic of a great technical achievement.

Chapter 12

Citizen of the World

Dr. Banting

After the towing trials of *HD-5* late in September, 1921, it became evident that Dr. Bell, then aged 74, was tiring. He took an ocean voyage to the Caribbean that winter, but it did not do much good. As 1922 rolled round, Bell appeared to be working as hard and with as much interest as ever. But time had taken its toll. For years he had fought against the diabetes which had plagued him. Gallant as he was, he could no longer resist it.

He tired noticeably as the summer wore on. Specialists were summoned from Washington, but they arrived too late. Alexander Graham Bell passed away during the night of August 2, 1922, at the age of seventy-five.

The funeral was simple but impressive. Mabel attended to her husband's final needs with loving care. Dr. Bell was clothed in his favourite tweed suit on which was pinned the Legion of Honour medal. His loyal colleagues carried him to the top of his beloved mountain for the last time. As he had requested, he was accompanied by joyful music.

Ironically, only a year after Bell's death, a young Toronto doctor named Frederick Banting saw his earlier experiments with insulin lead to a cure for diabetes.

Bell's beloved wife Mabel died on January 3, 1923, and was buried by his side.

Alexander Graham Bell was born in Scotland, travelled to Canada as a young man, and spent much of his life and creative energy in Ontario and Cape Breton. He became a citizen of the United States, but was in fact a citizen of the world. His inventions benefited people in every country.

Not only was his citizenship universal, but his experiments and creations covered the scientific spectrum. Furthermore, he was honoured by nearly every nation in the Western world.

He continued to give generously in return. His Volta Prize was converted into the Volta Laboratory and the Volta Bureau for the Deaf. He contributed to the Smithsonian Institute and he helped found the National Geographic Society.

Bell National Historic Park at Baddeck, Cape Breton, Nova Scotia

Today his works are exhibited from Baddeck to Brantford and from Montreal to Washington. A huge international company bears his name, a name which is synonymous with the telephone. Over a century after its development, the phone has become the basis for a multifaceted communications industry capable of connecting people instantaneously the world over, in ways perhaps glimpsed by the visionary genius of Alexander Graham Bell.

Dr. Bell and Helen Keller

Perhaps he is best remembered, however, by those silent hosts of deaf people in every country who recognize his humanity and his genuine concern for their plight. This may well be where his true memorial lives, residing in the hearts of grateful men and women to whom he gave the gift of speech.

Further Reading

Several brief studies of Bell's life and work are available for younger readers, including:

Dunn, Andrew. *Alexander Graham Bell*, Hove: Wayland, 1990.

James, Richard. *Alexander Graham Bell*, NY: Watts, 1990.

Joseph, Paul. *Alexander Graham Bell*, Minneapolis: Abdo, 1996.

Langille, Jacqueline. *Bell*, Tantallon: Four East, 1989.

Miller, Paul. *Alexander Graham Bell*, Agincourt: GLC, 1981.

Parker, Steve. *Bell and the Telephone*, NY: Chelsea House, 1995.

Quiri, Patricia. *Graham Bell*, NY: Watts, 1991.

Town, Florida. *Alexander Graham Bell*, Toronto: Grolier, 1988.

Webb, Michael. *Inventor of the Telephone*, Mississauga: Copp Clark Pitman, 1991.

More challenging and substantial studies include:

Boettinger, H. M. *The Telephone Book*, NY: Riverwood, 1977.

Bruce, Robert. *Bell and the Conquest of Solitude*, Boston: Little, Brown, 1973.

Costain, Thomas. *The Chord of Steel*, Garden City: Doubleday, 1960.

Davidson, Margaret. *The Story of Alexander Graham Bell*, Milwaukee: Gareth Stevens, 1989.

Eber, Dorothy. *Genius at Work*, Toronto: McClelland & Stewart, 1982.

Foster, Tony. *The Sound and the Silence*, Halifax: Nimbus, 1996.

Grosvenor, Edwin; Wesson, Morgan. *Alexander Graham Bell: The Life and Times*, NY: Abrams, 1997.

Mackay, James. *Alexander Graham Bell: A Life*, NY: Wiley, 1997.

Pasachoff, Naomi. *Alexander Graham Bell: Making Connections*, NY: Oxford, 1996.

Shippen, Katharine. *Bell Invents the Telephone*, NY: Random House, 1980.

St. George, Judith. *Dear Dr. Bell*, NY: Beech Tree, 1993.

In other media, titles include:

Alexander Graham Bell (CD-ROM), Sydney: Fitzgerald Studio, 1996.

For You Mr. Bell (video), Montreal: National Film Board, 1971.

The Sound and the Silence (video), Atlanta: Turner, 1992.

Credits

Alberta Government Telephones 38

Appleton-Century 42

Bell Canada 7, 15, 16, 20, 32, 34, 36, 38

Bell Family / National Geographic Society 8, 21, 28, 29, 45, 47, 48, 49, 50, 51, 53, 56, 58, 59, 60, 61, 63.

Bell National Historic Park 63

Brown, Son & Ferguson 13

Canada Post 9

Faber& Faber 52

Francis Antony 41

Information Canada 22

Jack Steiner 11, 25, 27

John Hancock 37

Library of Congress 44

Metro Toronto Public Library 3, 4, 5, 14, 17, 23, 39, 40

NYNEX Pioneers 18

Parks Canada 43, 50, 54, 55

Public Archives of Canada 18 (C70361), 31 (C 11334), 37 (PA28924), 52 (C28213), 57 (PA61741), 62 (C37756)

Index

Aerial Experiment Association 50-57
aircraft 47-57
Baddeck 43, 44, 46, 52, 57, 60, 63
Baldwin, Casey 51, 52, 54, 55, 58-61
Baldwin, Robert 51
Banting, Frederick 62
Beinn Bhreagh 43, 44, 47, 49
Bell, Alexander (grandfather) 7
Bell, Alexander Melville (father) 4-11, 15-21, 26-28, 37, 43
Bell, Chichester (cousin) 39
Bell, David (uncle) 35, 37
Bell, Edward Charles (brother) 4
Bell, Edward Ottoway (nephew) 5
Bell, Eliza Grace [Symonds] (mother) 8, 15, 17
Bell, Mabel [Hubbard] (wife) 20, 28, 30-32, 37, 43, 45, 49, 51, 62
Bell, Marion (daughter) 43, 45
Bell, Melville James (brother) 5, 10-12
Blake, Clarence 26
Boston 19, 20, 22, 23, 28, 33, 37
Brant, Joseph 17
Brantford 15, 17-19, 28, 31, 34, 35, 63
Brown, George 30
Chappe, Claude 14
Cros, Charles 40
Dom Pedro II 32-34
Curtiss, Glenn 51-57
Dunlop, George 35, 36
Edinburgh 4, 5, 7-9
Edison, Thomas 39-42
Ellis, Wallis 34, 35
Fuller, Sarah 19, 20
Garfield, James 44-45
Grand River 15, 17, 18, 27, 35
Gray, Elisha 24, 31, 33
Grosvenor, Elsie [Bell] (daughter) 8, 43, 45
Grosvenor, Melville Bell (grandson) 8, 50
Hargrave, Lawrence 49
hearing 19, 20, 22, 25-27, 32, 42, 51, 63
Helmholtz, Hermann von 23
Henderson, Thomas 6, 15, 17, 35
Henry, Joseph 33
Herdman, Ben 8-9
Hubbard, Gardiner Greene 20, 22, 23, 28, 30-32
Keller, Helen 21, 22, 63
Kempelen, Baron von 11-12
Lippincott, Jesse 42
London 4, 5, 13, 19, 20, 23, 61
Lord Kelvin 33
marine craft 58-61
McCurdy, John 51, 52, 55, 57, 58
McFarlane, Lewis 35
medicine 3-5, 44-46
Mercadier, Ernest 39
National Geographic Society 63
Paris (Ontario) 15, 35
phonograph 39-42
Queen Victoria 37
Reis, Johann 13, 23
Sanders, George 20-22
Selfridge, Thomas 50-52, 55, 57
Shakespeare, William 7, 34-37
speech 7, 8, 10, 11, 19, 20, 23, 25, 28, 63
Swinyard, Thomas 35
telegraph 13, 20, 23-26, 28, 30, 32, 35, 36
Tainter, Summer 39, 41, 42, 44
telephone 13, 22, 24, 28-42, 63
Thomson, William 33, 34
Traill, Catharine Parr 5
Tutelo Heights 17, 22, 28, 35
Volta Laboratories / Bureau 37, 39, 40, 42, 63
Washington 37, 43-46, 52, 61-63
Watson, Thomas 23, 29-31, 33, 34, 47
Wheatstone, Charles 13
White, Robert 35, 36
Williams, Charles 23
Wolfe, James 14
Wright Brothers 51, 56